JOKES AND HOW TO TELL THEM

Jokes

AND HOW TO TELL THEM

by Larry Adler

ILLUSTRATED BY ISADORE SELTZER

Doubleday & Company, Inc.,
Garden City, New York

'm no good at telling stories—I can never remember them."

You not only can't, you shouldn't try. The ending, the punch line should be all you need to remember. The ending should recall the story, which should be adapted to the audience at the time of telling. You rarely tell a story exactly the same way twice.

If you are an American, telling a purely American story to an Englishman, you must know your Englishman. Is he likely to understand American idiom? If not, you must edit the slang and translate it into international English, and if it is basically a good and funny story it will survive the translation with humor intact. No sense in using a phrase like "he shot him a fast curve on the inside" to someone who knows nothing of baseball.

If you are telling a story in English to, say, a Frenchman who speaks English well, you should still cut out idiom and slang as much as possible. You should slow down your normal speed of delivery and be sure that each word is clear and distinct. Or shout very loud, that'll make the bastard understand!

"Hey, whyncha look whehya gawn, f'krissake," is all right if you're telling a story using everyday Americanese to another American. But a Hindu, one with a good command of English, may be bewildered.

"Hey, why don't you look where you're going?" is clear. You lose some flavor but you can still convey a lot of inflection. Notice that in my translation I left out the "f'krissake." Unless you know your audience it's better to cut the slangy use of Christ's name. This isn't pedantry; use it if you're sure it's all right. If you're not sure, it may make you self-conscious and that will affect the telling.

This also applies to sexual and scatological terms. Occasionally such terms are necessary (though less often than you might think) and in such cases, if you tell the story, you need and must use the terms. It is a question of taste and good judgment. Never tell a story using the so-called "dirty" words just for shock value. That's just bad manners and stamps you as a boor. The reaction to your story should be a laugh, not a snigger, giggle or leer.* The test is: Would the story still be funny without the "words." If not, then you need them, but if the story *is* funny without them, cut them out. A good storyteller who knows his audience and is sensitive to atmosphere will never lapse into vulgarity.

* All legal points have been checked with Snigger, Giggle & Leer, my lawyers.

6

It is difficult, nearly impossible, to convey the humor of a religious story to an orthodox believer in that religion.

E. B. White in *The Elements of Style*, writing about a corny journalist, remarks, "He is tasteless, humorless (though full of fun)."

That pinpoints the Funny Fellow who likes to "talk dirty." He is not really telling a story so much as he is figuratively scrawling graffiti on lavatory walls. He does get laughs—from himself, above all, and from his like who equate smut with masculinity. If you don't think him funny, you are labeled a Bad Sport.

A good story should be logical, no matter how wildly improbable the premise. Animals don't talk (though I've heard about what goes on between dolphins—such *language!*) but if they do in your story, they should talk logically. Contrived stories, where situations are manipulated just to get a touch of bathroom or bed into it should be written off. No good.

Here is the definitive example of contrived humor.

The Lord Mayor of London, wearing his robes of office, is entertaining the Queen of Siam. She is wearing a low-cut gown and in the cleft of her bosom she wears a rose.

MAYOR: Would you blush if I plucked your rose?
QUEEN: Would you flush if I pulled your chain?

The story is an excellent yardstick for measuring humor response. It will often get a laugh, or titter, but is not really

7

funny. It assumes that flushing a toilet is funny *per se*. There is a wan smile, perhaps, in the double meaning of "pulled your chain,"—our Funny Fellow can stretch it out into a triple—the smile is even wanner in the rhyming of blush and flush. But the machinery creaks as all those unlikely props are hauled into place just to produce that double meaning. One thing in its favor—the meaning is at least double. Too many *double-entendres* remain sadly and hideously *single*. (pr. "sang-luh.")

I don't think the Funny Fellow would agree with any of this. Why, he is likely to say, why analyze humor anyway? If it gets a laugh, it's funny. Leave it at that: Why kill it by pulling it to bits?

I think it is important to analyze humor. (So did Freud and Bergson, among others.) But if you tell me what you laugh at, I can make a stab at telling you what you are (Adler's Law). Do you laugh at practical jokes, such as the hot foot, the exploding cigar and the dribble glass? Do you think it amusing to throw bags of water or urine out of hotel windows, to "goose" women with electric canes? Do you find it funny when a man puts on a lampshade or a woman's hat? Do you find automatic humor in harelips, deafness, stammering, lameness? (There is a difference between funny stories involving these conditions and the conditions themselves.)

If you believe that such things are funny in themselves,

you're reading the wrong book. To me humor is a subtle and subversive fellow, never wearing a uniform.

Here are some other points about stories and storytelling. As a general rule, but allowing for the brilliant exception, stories about Jews are best told by Jews. I have yet to hear an Englishman tell an American story well. The accent tends to be burlesqued, not imitated, and the result sounds malicious rather than funny. Pretty much the same case in reverse; both sides try too hard. The story becomes an exercise in propaganda and ceases to be funny. These points will come up again when I illustrate specific stories.

I suggest that before you tell any story involving a foreign national or a minority group you try to examine your motives. If you merely want to tell a story because you think it a funny one, fine. But if your Negro story helps the stereotyped legend of the Negro as a happy though rather stupid darky, forget it. Same with a Jewish story that makes the Jew the whining shoulder-shrugging Ikey who says "oy-oy." Dialect is really rather old-fashioned; whenever you can eliminate it, do. And *never* exaggerate it; you are sure to be offensive to someone in your audience when you do exaggerate.

What I am saying is that it is unfair to put your prejudices into a story. This is what Streicher did with his magazine *Die Stuermer*. Ostensibly a humor magazine, it portrayed faithfully the image of the Jew that Hitler wanted to project. The storyteller should be above such crude propaganda devices.

Now a word to the listener. Listening needs concentration, hard enough at any time but especially in a restaurant or at a party. A story is being told and you want to listen but when the waiter comes up, you switch attention to give your order. This switch may be short but it will be long enough to kill the story. You politely ask your friend to go on but he, if he is a good storyteller, knows that the story is now dead. It was killed by the interruption.

A card, large enough for the waiter to see, reading "Story In Progress" might help. It might help, but I doubt it. I am convinced that waiters have special training in story-interruption.

Another thing about listening: concentrate on the storyteller. If your eyes wander, say, to look at a painting or someone walking outside, that's bad enough. You should try not to. But what is worse is to begin whispering to your neighbor. This is real rudeness; you are almost saying in so many words that the story, or the teller, or both, is a bloody bore. And in fact this may be true but noblesse oblige, don't let it show. Also, try not to light a cigarette.

You, the listener, must never interrupt. Too many listeners interject remarks or cracks as something the storyteller has said brings up an association in their minds. The listener, as well as the teller, must be an editor. It requires will power to suppress that witticism at the moment it occurs but suppress it you should. One crack out of the listener breaks the continuity that a good story needs.

Then there is the fellow impatient for *your* story to finish so he can get *his* in. He starts preparing his story, loses the thread of the one you're telling; you have noted the semi-glazed look that indicates wandering attention and so your own enthusiasm is dampened and the story limps lamely away.

Many a storyteller asks you to stop him if you've heard it. He only half means it. He doesn't *want* to tell you a story you've already heard but he *does* want to tell the story. Should you stop him?

I say yes. If you are the sole audience, why waste his time and yours by letting him go on with it? Sometimes, of course, you don't realize until the halfway mark or later that you already know the story.

For that situation, plus the one where there are others listening, I nod and give what I hope is an appreciative smile, but which will show also that the story is a familiar one. If others are listening, the narrator can still go on but he knows that I will not, cannot, be surprised into laughter.

I can only laugh genuinely when I am surprised by the ending. A story that announces its finish in advance is apt to be dull. Also, it is almost insulting and certainly hypocritical to try faking a laugh. It usually sounds as phony as it is and the storyteller knows it at once.

There are types who never seem to listen at all. When the story is over—they know it's over because you've stopped talking—they react in strange ways. One way is to guffaw once, a strange mirthless bray which comes out as "*ah-HAHHHH!*"

Another type waits until the end, opens his mouth to denote incredulous admiration, points an almost accusative finger at you and says, "*Fun*-neee! I *like* that." Or else he just nods wisely but rather deadpan and intones, "That's fun-ny." I find these and similar robotlike reactions depressing.

At the Brown Derby in Hollywood, a group of writers sits at a round table every day for lunch. They tell stories all through lunch but no one ever really listens, each one waiting for the moment where he can jump in with *his* gag. One day a writer comes in, a bit later than the others, and sits down.

"Sam what's the matter with you," says one fellow, "you look awful!"

"Oh, it's just that I've had some really bad news. My wife's mother is dying and I've got to fly to New York right away. There's no plane before 3:30 so I'm just gonna grab a quick bite before I go out to the airport. But the way my wife sounded on the phone, I don't think there's a hope of me getting there before the old lady dies."

The first fellow says, "You think *that's* funny, listen to *this!*"

The fellow who has to catch a plane is serious, a bit dis-
trait as he tells the first writer what has happened. The
punch line is delivered excitedly, with a pointing finger.

A warning to listeners: let the other fellow's story get its
full laugh before you come in with your own nifty. This
means be sure that *everyone* has savored the joke and
laughed at it before you tell yours. I hate to be obvious but
let me repeat, *don't* step on the other fellow's laugh. You
sure as hell won't like it when it's done to you.

A cardinal sin is to announce that you know a quite similar story or else a different version of the same one you've
just heard and then proceed to tell it. Apart from the sheer
gracelessness of doing such a thing, the result is usually
that the same story is told twice.

Some people are compulsive about telling stories to pro-
fessionals, meaning either comedians or just show people in
general. This urge should be resisted unless the amateur is
very gifted. Of course there are many good amateurs but
they're seldom as good as the pros. And even someone in
show business who is not a good storyteller is still used to
hearing the experts. He grows restive at the amateur's ef-
forts.

A good story is a kind of one-act play, every detail helping
to propel the story to its curtain. The details that too many
storytellers lay on for atmosphere tend to slow the story
down. The best story contains not one wasted word.

Be sure that the details of the story are clear, including

proper names when needed. Fuzzy phrases like "such and such," "so and so," "one thing led to another," are very distracting. Any details that do not bear directly on the story, that do not help advance it to its conclusion, should be edited out. But those that remain should be remembered exactly so that, in telling the story, you should never have to fumble for a word, a phrase, a name.

Now for the stories. I will give you one that is guaranteed to work well with any group (assuming that they know English). You don't have to worry about offending anyone's sensibilities and the situation requires no expert knowledge from either teller or listener.

At La Scala, in Milan, a tenor is making his debut in *I Pagliacci*. When he sings the famous "Vesti la giubba" aria, the applause is so tremendous that they can't go on with the opera and he has to sing an encore. And again. In fact, he sings it eight times. Finally he steps to the footlights and waits until he gets complete silence from the audience.

"My friends," he says, "we have made history here tonight. I say 'we' because it is certainly you, the audience, as much as I. So far as I know, nobody in the history of La Scala, not Martinelli, not Schipa, not Gigli, not even *Caruso*, ever sang the 'Vesti la giubba' more than six times. And you, my dear friends, have caused me to sing it eight—it is the greatest moment of my singing career—I shall never forget it. But—there is still the rest of the opera to perform and my throat is becoming just a bit tired. So I ask you, dear friends, do not ask me to sing this aria again."

From the gallery:

"You'll sing it 'til you get it *right!*"

This story is a classic. The punch cannot be anticipated. Now first a warning: don't put on an Italian accent. We assume that he is an Italian singing and talking to an Italian audience, therefore he speaks the language without accent.

The description and dialogue that I set down is the way that I would be apt to tell it. I do not want you to ape me but for the time being, use my example as a model. If certain words or phrases seem unnatural to your own style or rhythm of speech, change them to suit yourself, but try to preserve the main structure of the story.

When the singer speaks to the audience, you, as the teller, must try to be that singer. Don't sluff off his speech in your anxiety to get to a sure-fire punch line. Make every phrase a part of the story.

He is humble; he says, with charming modesty, that credit for a sensational achievement is only partially his. The humility and modesty help to heighten the tension that is only released when the man from the gallery verbally gives him a good swift kick.

He dramatically builds a list of great singers who have failed to equal his own success; not Martinelli, not Schipa, not Gigli, not even Caruso, etc. He is profoundly moved as he hints that maybe he's greater than Caruso. He is endearing as he suggests that perhaps the rest of the opera is worth hearing and that he should be excused from another encore.

The man in the gallery should cup his hands to his mouth and bellow the punch line.

The violinist, Ysaÿe, does a recital tour through Sweden and has in his program the Bach Chaconne. In a small town near Uppsala, he looks through the curtain and sees that his audience seems to be mainly hicks—farmers in overalls —so he decides that the Chaconne would be wasted on them and he plays something lighter. After the concert a farmer comes to the dressing room and says:

"Mr. Ysaÿe, I traveled fifty kilometers in my horse and cart just to hear you, and you didn't play the Chaconne."

Ysaÿe says, "My dear man, I had no idea that anyone here would either know or give a damn whether I played the Chaconne or not. Come back with me to my hotel, we'll have dinner and afterward I shall give you a private concert."

They go back and after dinner, a liqueur and a good cigar, Ysaÿe gets up, takes out his Amati violin and plays the Chaconne. When he finishes, the farmer says:

"Well, well, well, so that's the Chaconne. You know, Mr. Ysaÿe, that's the first time I ever heard it. I don't like it."

You notice that I use the present tense. Ysaÿe "does" a tour rather than "did" a tour. Perhaps because a story is a process of continuous action, it is better to use "he says" instead of "he said." This holds true for most stories, no matter how far back in time the scene is set.

Remember, these stories are written to be told rather than to be read to oneself. The phrases, verb tenses, etc. are meant for speaking, and anything that does not contribute directly to advancing the story is cut out. Each story is, in a sense, a one-act play.

Now one assumes that Ysaÿe and the farmer are speaking Swedish to each other and therefore no accent is needed for either character.

On the farmer's first line, he is diffident before the great man, yet brave enough to complain about the Chaconne having been cut out. Ysaÿe is open, cordial, the great musician happy at the idea of finding a kindred soul in a hick town.

There are two danger points in the farmer's last lines. You are liable to get laughs after "so that's the Chaconne" and also after "that's the first time I ever heard it." These are unwanted laughs and can ruin the story. Try to get over these danger points in the following manner.

Study the farmer's final speech, which, by the way, is not easy to deliver. His "well, well, well," should sound satisfied and happy. He is confidential as he warms up to his final point. In delivering the last part, don't come to any kind of stop until the very end. He shakes his head admiringly (all of this is a false clue, of course) as he says, "so that's the Chaconne." There should be a pause but almost an imperceptible one after "that's the first time I ever heard it." If you make a full stop there, people will think that's the end of the story and start to laugh politely. You must cover that pause and go right on to "I don't like it" before anyone has time to laugh.

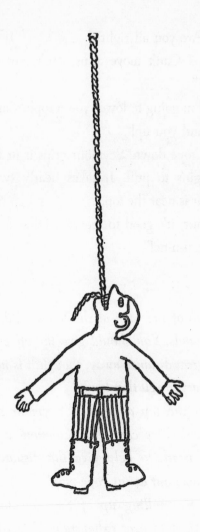

Two fellows are mountain climbing. One of them is about fifty feet above the other. He suddenly loses his grip and falls about two thousand feet and lands spread-eagled in the snow. His friend looks out over the precipice and yells:

"Seymour! Are you all right?"

"I'm fi-ii-iine! Can't move arms, can't move legs, otherwise, fi-ii-iine!"

"Seymour! I'm going to lower you a rope. Catch it in your teeth. I will haul you up!"

So he lets a rope down, Seymour grips it in his teeth and the friend begins to pull. It takes nearly two hours but finally Seymour is near the top.

"Ah, Seymour, it's good to see you, fella—how are you?"

"I'm FI-II-ɪɪ-ɪɪ-ii-ne!"

The dialogue of the man at the top should be delivered with cupped hands. You should give the effect of shouting to someone a great distance away, though it is not, of course, actually necessary to yell that loud.

The man at the top as well as Seymour should speak very slowly, with very careful articulation, a slight pause between each word, to help give the distance effect. "A rope" should come out as "ay rope-puh."

Pantomime the pulling up of Seymour to convey the great effort leading to near exhaustion. The friend is worn out but happy as he gets Seymour near enough to speak to him without shouting.

Seymour's final answer should be normal on "I'm" then rising to a shriek and gradual fadeaway on "FI-II-ɪɪ-ɪɪ-ii-ne!"

The "I'm," though said in normal tones, should be said very quickly so that you jump at once to the shriek.

If your timing is good, you can throw in a shriek near the beginning to dramatize Seymour's first fall.

After I first heard this story it was nearly two weeks before I could tell it without breaking up myself. To break up, to laugh at your own story, is one of the deadlier sins, but maybe this example just shows how sadistic I am.

A young man is talking to his mother.

"Mumsie," he says, "I want to have a long talk with you. You've probably noticed that my friendship for Marvin has become—how shall I say—well, it's ripened into something rich and sincere and true and good. Well, Mumsie, I love Marvin and Marvin loves me. We wish to announce our engagement and that's what this talk is about."

"Son," the mother says, "do you realize what you're saying?"

"Oh indeed, Mumsie, indeed I do. That's just why I've come to you; we've always been chums, Mumsie, you and I, none of this silly silver cord jazz. We wish to announce our engagement but of course I wouldn't dream of making even a move without your blessing."

"But son—think what people will say—you cannot go against convention—"

"Oh, Mumsie, you're going to be dreary, I can feel it coming on. I never would have thought it of you, Mumsie, of all people. Well, very well, let's have it out. What possible objection could anyone have to my marrying Marvin?"

"He's Jewish!"

I love this story because it illustrates, as does no other story I know, the flimsy support behind the façade of prejudice. Now, since the story involves a homosexual, restraint is the watchword. The camping should be implied rather than demonstrated.

There is no need of an exaggerated lisp or flamboyant gestures. A slight accent on the sibilants is enough. Very few hand gestures and keep them natural.

Sonny is just a bit exasperated at Mumsie's reactionary attitude and perhaps a faint touch of camp can come in. But keep it faint. One touch of roaring queen and your story is destroyed by vulgarity.

Mumsie should be agitated at the news but she should be sweetly reasonable as she says her final line.

*Sonny interrupts her second speech and there is no need after each character is identified to say, "he says" or "she says." The dialogue indicates clearly enough just who is speaking.**

* One queer says to another, "I've just read an article in a medical journal. It says that sleeping with women gives you *lung* cancer."

The other queer says, "I don't *believe* it. I mean, I just don't *think* that's *true.*"

"Well," the first one says, "*actually* you're quite right. It *isn't* true. But *spread* it around."

A mother takes her son to the Rijksmuseum in Amsterdam. She stops before a Rembrandt painting of the Nativity, Mary in the manger with the infant Jesus.

"Look at this painting, Stanley," she says, "and remember it well. A typical example of Gentile mentality. Money for a *hotel* room she hasn't *got* but she can have her *portrait* painted."

I specify which art gallery and which painter. Vagueness about such details merely confuses the listener. There's a world of difference between saying "one of the well-known art galleries" and "a painting by so-and-so, you know, one of the famous painters." Woolly phrases can ruin your story before you reach the main point.

An old Jew is dying. His wife sits by his bedside and there is a terrible storm outside. Suddenly there is a wide streak of lightning followed by a terrific clap of thunder. The old man sits up and says:

"I'm about to die. Send for a priest."

"Sam," his wife says, "not only you're dying, you're also losing your mind. Surely you mean a rabbi?"

The man says, "A rabbi should go out on a night like this?"

In both of the last two stories a Yiddish accent is unnecessary. The sentence construction, based on Yiddish thinking (or German, for that matter) established the character without having to add dialect. The "Vell, I'll tell you," stereotype is out, so is the rather nauseating whine and shoulder-shrugging without which no Jewish story was complete. Don't need it any more.

There is a temptation to lay on the details in such a story as this last one. I advise you to install a stern editor just behind the cerebrum and have him censor eighty-five per cent of practically everything.

You might want to draw out the drama of the dying man with wheezes, gasps and groans, not to mention the sobs and moans of the widow-to-be. Leave them out. When I write, "'Sam,' his wife says," that's just the way I'd tell it. She would "say," not "sob brokenheartedly, tears streaming down her face." (Tears should stream up?)

When her husband announces that he is about to die, he need do so only in normal tones. His wife should sound anxious but not stricken—despite the subject, the story isn't morbid and shouldn't be made to sound that way. But the man's final answer should have dramatic vigor. He doesn't mind dying but he is outraged at the idea of inconveniencing a rabbi.

A man is sitting in the living room, reading the paper. His wife says, "Sidney, close the window. It's cold outside."

He pays no attention.

"Sidney, would you mind please to close the window? It's cold outside."

No answer. He goes on reading.

"Sidney, this is the third time I've had to ask you. Would you *please* close the window—it's *cold* outside."

Sidney gets up, goes to the window, slams it shut, and says:

"So now it's *warm* outside?"

A faint suggestion of Yiddish accent can be used here. The "w" in "window" leans toward a "v" sound but not broad or hard. More like the "v" used in a Castilian accent in Spanish. While I have italicized "please" and "cold" on the wife's third request, I mean that these should be stressed but by no means shouted. Her exasperation mounts

29

at each request but remains controlled. Sidney's only line should be sardonic, not heavily sarcastic, which would spoil the line. He is annoyed and irritated but doesn't lose his temper.

A customer at a Jewish restaurant is so well known as a borscht lover that whenever he comes in they immediately serve him borscht without bothering to take his order. One day, after being served, he beckons to the waiter.

"Waiter," he says, "taste the borscht."

"You don't like it?"

"Taste it."

"Look, you don't like, so I'll change it."

"Taste it."

"Why do I have to taste? You don't like? So I'll give you a menu, you'll select something else, I'll bring already and no extra charge. We only want to please you."

"Taste the borscht!"

"Look, I got fifty-seven other customers here, I'm gonna taste everybody's borscht, I won't get any work done!"

The customer stands up.

"Will you sit *down* and *taste* the BORSCHT!"

The waiter sits down, looks around the table.

He says, "So where's the spoon?"

The customer goes, "Ah-*hah!*"

I'm now in the position of the pimp at Aden who catches a Yankee tourist as he comes off the gangplank. He offers him "nice young girl, nine years old, virgin," and when the tourist refuses, he offers "nice young boy, also virgin, very pretty," and the tourist gets mad. "Dammit," he yells, "I don't want a nice young girl or a nice young boy. Goddammit, I want the American consul!"

The pimp murmurs, "Very difficult, but I try."

All right, so I'll try. This is a difficult story to tell. The customer is bland, smiling, patient, and only when he stands up is he forceful, faintly menacing, gesturing with emphasis as he says, "Will you sit down and taste the BORSCHT."

The waiter, at first good-humored, grows agitated at the

32

customer's persistence and near boiling point when he complains about his fifty-seven other customers.

When he reluctantly sits down, conveying through his resigned manner that he is dealing with an old friend turned madman, he looks around the table rather helplessly as he says, "So where's the spoon?"

The climax is harder than the telling. I feel that the customer should switch back to his former affability as he lifts a finger and says, gently, "Ah-hah."

And even with "ah-hah" I'm making a concession. I would rather end it with a murmured "ah." However I find it impossible to convey the degree of inflection in print.

And opinions differ on this ending. Isaac Stern and Jack Benny both prefer an admonishing "ah-hah" or even "Ah-HAH!" I wish they'd both stick to their fiddle playing.

In '29, after the stock market crash, banks were failing all over the place. On the Lower East Side of New York there was a man walking up and down in front of one such bank, shaking his fist at the closed doors and muttering to himself:

"In the electric chair, they should put such people. In the electric chair, those people in there. They should hang by the neck 'til they're *dead*, those people. President, vice-president, chairman, board of directors, everybody, they should put on a guillotine and chop off the *heads*, those people in there."

"Gangsters, mobsters, they should be put in a cement mixer, they should all be ground up and come out *hamburgers*, those people in there."

A cop walks up to him.

"What're you so excited about, Mac—did you have dough in that bank?"

The man says, "*I didn't have. If I had. AH!*"

You need an accent but be careful with it. This is no "Vell, I'll tell you" type of fellow. He is an endearing humanitarian, outraged at injustice even when he's not the victim. His bloodthirsty curses are hyperbolic, not what he really feels, like that wonderful Yiddish malediction, "It should grow inside your stomach a trolley-car!"

The cop is straight New York cop.

On "I didn't have," the man points to himself. On "If I had," he points his finger and gestures like an emphatic lecturer. On "AH," he lifts his head a bit and repeats, with even more emphasis the lecturing gesture. The final sound he makes is hard to reproduce accurately. It isn't quite "ah," nor is it "oh," but something between the two, like "Aw!" What he is saying, of course, is that if you think this is getting excited, you should see if I really had money in that bank, would I give a geshrei (a scream of rage)!

Old lady in the subway, shawl over her head, looking around her rather helplessly. She thinks she spots a friendly face, goes up to a man and says:

"*Kennst reden Yiddish?*"

"What'd you say, lady?"

"*Feh!*" She goes up to another man.

"*Kennst reden Yiddish?*"

"I'm sorry, madam, I didn't quite understand you—would you mind repeating that?"

"*Feh!*" She goes up to a third man.

"*Kennst reden Yiddish?*"

"*Ya, mamaleh, ich sprecht Yiddish.*"

"*Aiee, Gott sie dank—zogt mir—*what time is it?"

Warn your audience in advance that even if they don't know Yiddish, they will by the end of the story, so don't interrupt. She is asking each man "Can you speak Yiddish?" and her "Feh!" at the barbaric Goyim is a growl of disgust, contrasted to her meek approach as she asks the question. When she finds a lantzman (a countryman) she is tearfully happy as she thanks God. Then the punch of her question delivered in clear articulate English without accent.

Once she starts to speak, no identifying words are necessary, as it is obvious who speaks each line.

Use the Yiddish "r," partially rolled but less broad than the Scots "brr."

The story was told to me by Stella (no relation) Adler, one of the few who has the really grand manner. One day in the early forties she went in to Cartier's to have a jewel re-set. The clerk, impressed by her clear articulation, said:

"Things must be very difficult for you in England just now."

Stella drew herself up, one of the better theatrical sights of our day.

"Ay'm not British," she said, "Ay'm just affected!"

On Christmas Eve, in New York, at the corner of Sixth Avenue and 52nd Street, a man is begging in the street. A fellow comes along, full of holiday spirit and hands the beggar a twenty-dollar bill. The beggar looks at the bill, turns around and tears up 52nd Street. The man, surprised, follows him and sees the beggar rush into "21." By the time the man gets there himself, checks his coat, he has lost sight of the beggar. He finally finds him at a table eating caviar.

"You sonofabitch," says the man. "I give you twenty bucks, that's probably more dough than you've seen in a year, and you go and blow it on caviar."

The beggar says, "Look, when I haven't got money, I can't eat caviar. When I've *got* money, I mustn't eat caviar. *When can I eat caviar?*"

The benefactor sounds bitter at the betrayal of his charity. The beggar, like the fellow outside the bank, is a gentle man, reacting to an unfair accusation. On his final sentence his voice rises in a scream of protest and he gestures with both hands to emphasize his indignation.

One detail that seems unimportant must not be left out. That is, "checks his coat." I have said that a story must follow logically from its premise. Checking the coat creates more time for the beggar not only to get to a table but to order and be served. If the listener's concentration is arrested by an illogical point in the story, you've lost him.

Two men go for the first time to the Colony Restaurant. At the end of the meal the waiter puts two little pewter bowls in front of them, each bowl with a rose petal floating in it.

"So what's that?" one asks.

"I don't know. You didn't order it?"

"So who ordered? Me, I'm gonna ask the waiter."

"Don't, Max—don't ask—you'll just look like a greenhorn."

"So I'll look. I didn't order, I don't want to pay. Waiter! Could you tell me please, what these things are?"

"Those, sir, are finger bowls. We put them there for you to dip your fingers in."

"You see, Max? You give him a silly question, he gives you a silly answer."

Again, no need for identifying remarks after the first "one asks." The dialogue points up each speaker.

Have you heard Moussorgsky's Pictures at an Exhibition? One piece is descriptive of two Jews, one deep bass

41

and confident, the other protestingly timid, with a high voice. Well, that's these two. Max has an air of authority, nobody's going to put anything over on him. His friend is Caspar Milquetoast, anything is better than making a scene.

And Caspar doesn't really enjoy his victory over Max. He doesn't even think he has won a point. Rather, he is saying unhappily, "I wish you hadn't done it."

The waiter should sound just a shade British.

Two men are compiling a Yiddish-English dictionary. They're on the "D's" and arrive at the word "disappointed." Neither of them can think of the Yiddish for that word.

"Look," says one of them, "I'll call my mother. She only speaks Yiddish and if anybody will know the word, she will."

So he phones his mother and says to her, in Yiddish, "Momma, you know I'm coming to dinner with you Friday night, like I do every Friday night. But suppose I phoned you on Friday, just before dinnertime and said to you that I had to stay at the office, that I couldn't come to dinner. What would you be?"

"Aiee, Boitrem, ah *zay* disappointed!"

Obviously you won't actually speak Yiddish when the man is speaking to his mother. (Unless you can, and your audience understands it, in which case, good luck to you.) Son will have no accent in his English when speaking to

Momma. Momma, naturally, will speak Yiddish, because the words are simple, almost cognate words, meaning "so disappointed!" And her word "disappointed" will have a Yiddish accent.

A woman goes to a spiritualist, a medium, she wants to get in touch with the spirit of her husband. The medium goes into a trance and after a while a voice comes out.

"Jonquil," it says, "are you there?"

"That's Benny," the wife says, "I'd know his voice anywhere. Benny—tell me—are you all right?"

"I'm fine, Jonquil."

"Tell me, Benny—where you are—it's nice?"

"Jonquil, is absolutely gorgeous. The sky is rather a cerulean blue. There are a few nimbus clouds—mein favorite type clouds. And the cows. Jonquil, I wish you could see those cows. Brown cows, white cows, black and white cows, speckled cows—such beautiful cows I've never seen, never in my whole life."

"Benny—I didn't know they had cows in heaven."

"Who's talking about *heaven?* I'm a *bull* in Argentina!"

I want to remind you that you are not bound to my dialogue nor my names. I'm writing these down just the way I would tell them, and they are written to be spoken rather than to be read. And at that, I wouldn't tell any given story exactly the same way twice. I allow a little leeway for improvisation, depending on my audience. You may not like the name "Jonquil." I do, but that's just personal choice. Some lines tend to stick; I am perhaps overfond of the phrase, "nimbus clouds—mein favorite type clouds" so no matter how I tell the story, those nimbus clouds are right in there.

Use a few light moans and hums when the medium goes into her trance. Benny might sound a bit sepulchral at first but he progresses to sounding calm and peaceful, rather like Sam Jaffe as the Grand Lama in Lost Horizon. Jonquil is excited, but trying to control herself, to keep calm for Benny. Benny begins to sound a shade less other-worldly as he works up enthusiasm in his description of the cows. He is human, right down-to-earth and with some asperity on the last line.

Two fellows meet on Fifth Avenue.

"What's *wrong* with you," says one, "you look *ghastly*. Are you *ill?*"

"You may *well* ask," says the other, "I feel my *whole* world's just come apart at the *seams*. Cedric has left me— just *skipped*, and with my entire wardrobe. I mean to say, I haven't a *stitch* except what's on my back. I've been *dismissed* at Bonwit's—got the sack, and just *try* to find a good window-decorating job these days. Plus which, my lease is up and I've *got* to be out of my flat by Sunday. *Honestly*, what with one thing and another. I was thinking *just* this morning—and *don't* you try to dissuade me, either—that the only way out is *suicide*. I'm going to do away with myself."

The other one says, "I'm *amazed* at you, absolutely *amazed*. Such *sheer* pessimism and from *you* of all people. So *gay*, so *debonair*, the *life* of the party, that's what *everyone* says about you. Now I'm going to make a suggestion. I want you to *pray*. I *mean* it, pray to *God*. *She'll* help you."

Again, no wrist-flapping or lisping. The language identi-fies the type. When in doubt, understate. Also, when not in doubt.

I assume you'll know your audience well enough to judge whether or not to tell this one. You can't joke to a dogmatist. (I resisted, rather manfully, the impulse to write "this kind of joke shouldn't happen to a dogmatist.") Dogma aside, this story is perfectly logical.

The ultra-modern twist to this story is the space-flier who returns to earth and says he's seen God. "And first of all, fellows, She's black."

The same situation as the last story. You can use the same opening. Then:

"I've been *fired*."

"Fired? *You*? But they *can't* fire you—why, you're Pepsi-Cola's *ace* sky-writer!"

"Nevertheless."

"Well, what happened? *Tell.*"

"A *grisly* business, all of it. Last Fourth of July I was commissioned to write 'Pepsi-Cola' *clear* across Manhattan, an ambition I'd harbored for *years*. I had a *divine* new plane and an absolutely *dreamy* fuel mixture which made perfect smoke—but *perfect!* And it was a *gorgeous* day. Well, I went up, wrote 'Pepsi' and then flew off about three miles just to take a *look*. You know me—I'm not one to brag, but I tell you, it was an *absolute* Rembrandt. Well, I was just going to fly back to dot the 'i' when a *nasty* flock of B-36 bombers flew right through and just *wrecked* my design. *Ruined* it. I was absolutely *livid*. I was so mad that I flew behind a cloud, wrote '*drat*'—and they *caught* me!"

My previous warnings about exaggerating the queer mannerisms still hold good. Underplay, it's always better than overplaying.

Curiously, when one says "a homosexual" it seems to be true that only the male is being described. Humor about the female is almost non-existent; here is the only example I've found.

"Mama, what's a Lesbian?"

"What do you mean, what's a—that's the most awful thing

—what's a Lesbian, indeed! You just wait 'til your stepfather gets home. Ask her!"

Still another warning: When you tell a homo story there's always the joyboy who says, "You tell those stories a little too well." There is nothing to be done about joyboy.

The Philadelphia Orchestra is having a rehearsal. During a coffee break a man comes in and introduces himself to the orchestra manager.

"Mr. McDonald," he says, "I'd like to audition for you. I happen to be a first-class player on every single instrument in the orchestra. Will you listen to me?"

McDonald says, "I'm sure you're all you say you are but I'm terribly sorry, there is no place open for you. Matter of fact there is a long waiting list of musicians who want to get into this orchestra."

The man says, "At least listen!" He picks up a violin and whips into Paganini's Twenty-fourth Caprice. Some of the musicians begin to nod—this fellow is good.

When he finishes McDonald says, "Look—you're very good indeed—I didn't doubt it. But as I explained to you, there is no room for you in the orchestra."

"Will you give me a chance and just listen!" the man yells. He grabs a viola and goes through the cadenza of the Walton Concerto. The musicians applaud and some even say, "Bravo!"

"Why do you do this?" says McDonald. "You're wasting your time and mine. It's not a question of your talent, there simply is no room—"

"For God's sake, just *wait* a minute and *listen!*" He leaps to a double-bass and goes into the rapid finale of Tchaikovsky's Fourth Symphony.

"Dammit," McDonald shouts, "how many times do I have to say it? I don't *care* how well you play, it doesn't *matter* how well you play, I'm trying to tell you there simply is *no* place for you in the orchestra at *all!*"

The man, absolutely exhausted, says, "Well I'll be a dirty sonofabitch!"

McDonald says, "Hey, that's different, we can always use a *conductor!*"

The tempo of delivery should speed up with each re-action by the man to McDonald's rejection. McDonald, at first courteous, gets madder and more impatient until he is almost violently angry after the double-bass solo. But he calms down suddenly and there is joy in his voice as he finally makes the man an offer.

You should also pantomime the musicians nodding approval and convey their mounting appreciation of the man's virtuosity.

The virtuoso himself should sound tired but not quite defeated as he gives up trying to impress.

You may decide to use a different orchestra and manager, depending on where you happen to be telling this story. You may want to select different instruments for the virtuoso to play but if so then you must choose works to match those instruments. The details must be absolutely authentic and each work clearly specified and committed to memory. There must be no fumbling for details in the telling. The listener should feel almost as if he were present at the audition.

A man has an obsessional dream through several years, that he is a great violinist. Actually he can't play at all but this dream keeps coming up. One day, in London, he is walking down Bond Street and comes to Hill's, the famous violin-makers. Suddenly the memory of the dream hits him and he walks in and says to the clerk:

"Excuse me, could I see one of them fiddle things?"

The clerk gets out a violin and shows it to him.

"I'd like to look at the stick, too."

The clerk hands him a bow, the man draws the bow across the strings and finds himself playing the Joachim cadenza of the Beethoven concerto.

The clerk says, "Excuse me, sir, but are you a concert artist?"

The man says, "Me? Nah, I ain't never touched one of these things before."

The clerk excuses himself, goes off and calls the Harold Holt Concert Bureau and asks if Ian Hunter, the director, could come over at once. Hunter comes over, listens to the man and says:

"Sir, I don't know who you are but you could do me a great service. Francescatti has just canceled for this Saturday at Festival Hall. He was to play the Beethoven but he's got a bursitis—could you possibly take his place?"

"Sure, what the hell," the man says.

So he gives the concert and it's a sensation. Cardus writes in the *Guardian* that this is the finest musical surprise since the young Menuhin. Hunter books a whole European tour for the man. He's giving a concert in Geneva at the same time that a summit conference is going on. Kennedy and Khrushchev both go to the concert and during the interval Khrushchev says:

"Look, how can two politicians like us disagree about anything after such beautiful music and great artistry?"

They make a public announcement that all major points are settled between them and they give the violinist due credit. Now the UN asks him to do a tour. He agrees and wherever he goes, peace breaks out. He plays in Cairo and the next morning Nasser calls Ben-Gurion on the phone.

"Benny, howsa boy? Look Benny, baby, howsabout a little lunchee, hey? Tomorrow? I'll send a plane for you, baby."

He plays in Nairobi and all the Mau-Mau troubles quieten down at once. He's back at his hotel, he has a room on the ground floor, and late at night he hears a scratching at his window. He opens it and there's a lioness.

"I *do* hope you'll excuse me," the lioness says, "I'm *dreadfully* sorry to disturb you so late at night, but you *know* how it is with us lions, they're *not* very tolerant here about letting us walk through town in daylight, I'm sure you *do* understand. Well, why I'm here is, we jungle folk are simply *dying* to hear your *wonderful* music. We couldn't *possibly* meet your fee but we've heard *ever so much* about your generosity—you artists are always *so* generous—and I've got about two hundred of us from our ladies' auxiliary out in the jungle just *hoping* and *praying* that you'll come. Could you *possibly*—"

"Sure," the violinist says, "what the hell. Wait, I'll get my fiddle."

So he gets the violin, climbs out of the window and follows the lioness out into the jungle. There are about two hundred animals, all kinds, sitting in a semicircle. The minute the man starts to play a snake starts rubbing noses with a mongoose, a coyote and a sheep snuggle close together, a tiger starts to nuzzle a cow. Suddenly a panther leaps out of a tree, jumps on the violinist, eats him up, eats the violin, eats the bow, everything.

The lioness goes up to the panther.

"What did you want to *do* that for? This man was just giving us a concert—for *free,* too—and you have to do such a thing. This *beautiful* music and you have to go and *ruin* it. *Why?*"

The panther (cupping a hand to his ear) goes, *"Eh?"*

This is a gem among musical stories. Don't waste it. Pick your audience very carefully. Also, before you tell it, make sure that you're completely confident about the many details so that you won't have to stop and search your memory for what comes next.

The story, if well told, is very hard to follow and few people would even try, so save it for the big moment. Don't tell it at the beginning of the evening. On the other hand, if you're at all ill at ease with the story, you'll lose your audience very quickly and the story will fizzle out long before the punch.

The violinist has a kind of Brooklyn accent, in contrast to the music he plays. He's a good-natured slob, surprised at nothing, will say yes to anything.

The lioness should sound rather like the local DAR chairman, leaning hard on the adverbs and speaking with the toothy smile that Joyce Grenfell, if you've ever seen her, manages so wonderfully when she impersonates clubwomen. This smile is ever-present and vanishes only in her speech to the panther. Here she is indignant, expostulating, almost tearful.

The panther should be a rather crotchety type, annoyed that his deafness gets in the way of hearing what the lioness is saying. He cups his ear like an old man as he half-quavers, "Eh?"

Two men are in a railway compartment in England. A man comes in, he's wearing a clerical collar, gaiters—he sits down and opens up a copy of the *Church of England News*.

One of the two men whispers, "Blimey, I know that geezer. 'E's the Archbishop of Canterbury."

The other man says, "Gahh."

"No, really, it's 'im, I seen 'im on the telly. It's the Archbishop, all right."

The second man says, "Gahh, 'at ain't the Archbishop. 'E's got 'is own private car and chauffeur, 'e wouldn't come walkin' into no third-class compartment sittin' down with the likes of us!"

"Bet a quid?"

"Okay, a quid. Go on, ask him."

The man gets up and walks over to the stranger.

"Excuse me—I don't mean to interrupt you, you reading your paper and all—but me and me friend there, we've got a little bet on. I say you're the Archbishop, see, and he says you ain't. You the Archbishop, eh?"

The man lowers his paper and says, "Bugger off."

The fellow goes back to his friend.

"Was it him?"

" 'E wouldn't say."

This one does need a Cockney flavor but don't try it unless you have had some experience with it. Any non-Englishman trying to do Cockney is in real trouble. For example, a Cockney saying "I say" does not come out as "Hoye sye." The dropped "h" is quite usual but the added one is pretty rare. The word "paper" is nearer to "piper" than "poyper." Both men talk sotto-voce to each other though the volume rises a bit as each challenges the other. But when the first man addresses the cleric, he's smarmy, cap-in-hand and rather unctuous. This points up the cleric's rude "Bugger off." Also, pantomime the cleric lowering his paper and glowering at the man. The first man delivers his punch line rather with a virtuous air. The second man's "Gahh" is a throaty growl of disgusted skepticism. Why don't you practice that one right now?

Again, here is a story with a danger point. People are liable to laugh after "Bugger off," thinking that's the end of the story. If it were, in fact, the end, it wouldn't be worth telling. You have to get in quickly with the line, "The fellow goes back to his friend," in order to kill off any chances of the unwanted laugh.

A man goes up to the guard on the dock at Southampton. "'Scuse me, cock, where's the urinal?" "It sailed this mornin'."

That's about the shortest good story I know but even so, it needs some explaining. The point depends on "urinal" being mispronounced so that it comes out "u-rye-nal," rather as if it were HMS Urinal. The guard is dour, humorless. His deadpan voice intones, "It sayled this moornin'."

In a very narrow street in London a Rolls and a Daimler approach each other and come to a stop. Neither can pass the other. The chauffeur of the Rolls puts his head out and says:

"Would you mind making way for 'Er Majesty, Queen Wilhelmina, Queen of Holland, Empress of the Netherlands and the Dutch East Indies Empire, *if you please?*"

The other chauffeur doesn't reply. He just gets out of the Daimler and opens the rear door to reveal Queen Mary.

"And *this*, I suppose, is a bag of *manure?*"

The story is out-of-date, in that it concerns the old Queen Mary and Queen Wilhelmina. Still, I keep them as the main characters because the last line is only explosive—which it is if told well—if you imagine the quite awful dignity of the old Queen.

The first chauffeur is icily polite, enunciating each word with Cockney carefulness. Try to imagine the late Charles Laughton telling that one. The second chauffeur is equally careful in his enunciation but more genial, even smiling with excessive courtesy as he delivers his knockout punch. I like to give the second chauffeur a bass voice with a kind of growl in it. And his very last word is spoken on a rising note of inquiry.

For me the story is made by the "I suppose." Without that qualifier it would lack a lot. Both chauffeurs speak slowly.

A rabbi goes into a ten-day fast, never leaving the synagogue. At the end of that time he sees a vision and believes that he is speaking directly to God.

"God, only you can help me in my terrible predicament. My son is about to turn Christian."

And God says, *"Your* son!"

No dialect or accent needed. And God, at least in this story, is just another exasperated Yiddish father.

A *shatchen*, a Jewish marriage broker, arranges with a family to bring over a girl that he thinks is a fine match for their son. After dinner, the girl leaves and the family immediately begins to attack the *shatchen*.

"What kind of girl you're bringing here? A monster! One eye in the middle of her forehead, the left ear way up here, the right ear way down there, and the chin goes way back here . . ."

The *shatchen* says, "Look, look, either you *like* Picasso or you don't."

First, shatchen *is a Jewish word and the "ch" is like the Scottish "ch" in "loch." You use pantomine, of course, as the family describes the girl's eye, ears and lack of chin. After "way back here" the* shatchen *interrupts. He speaks protestingly, wearily. He raises his hands in a defensive attitude as he says, "Look, look," and these words are uttered slowly, though he speeds up a bit on the rest of the sentence.*

A traveler, in Shanghai, asks at his hotel if there is a synagogue in town.

"It's Rosh Hashana, the Jewish New Year," he says, "and I'd like to go to synagogue if there's one in town."

"Oh yes," the clerk tells him, "we have one that is over fifteen hundred years old—one of our landmarks."

He tells the traveler where to go, the traveler goes to the synagogue and stays there all day for the religious service. At the end of the day the rabbi of this Shanghai synagogue comes up to him.

"Tell me, please," the rabbi says, "you American? You English?"

"I'm English, actually," the man says.

"Ah, so? Tell me please, why you like visit our synagogue?"

"Why? Because it's Rosh Hashonah, that's why. I always go to shule on Rosh Hashonah."

"So! You mean, you Jew?"

"Of course I'm a Jew."

"Ah, so; ah, so—very interesting—you know, you no *look* Jew!"

I've raised the point many times about not overdoing dialect. It especially applies here. Remember, the rabbi is Chinese, not a chink-chink Chinaman in a corny laundry joke.

So therefore, no pidgin-type cutesiness. The Chinese do tend to make the "l" sound out of the letter "r" but even so, don't have the rabbi say, "you Amellican?" Also, don't add any "ee" suffixes to words. I have never heard a Chinese say, "No tickee, no shirtee" in my life.

Not everyone gets the point of this one right away. Wait for it. If it misses, let it go. All Jews look alike, everybody knows that, and that's why the Chinese rabbi is surprised that this white man is a Jew.

A man goes to see the doctor. The doctor asks him what's wrong.

"Nothing much, really," the man says, "just that I'm dead."

"Oh," says the doctor, "that's very interesting. Dead, eh?"

The doctor goes on talking for a while, then says:

"By the way, did you know that dead people don't bleed?"

"No," says the man, "that's new to me."

"Well, it's quite logical," the doctor says, "you see, when someone is dead—like you—the heart stops and therefore the blood is no longer pumped through the arteries."

"Yeah, sure, I see that. That makes sense."

Suddenly the doctor jabs the man's thumb with a pin. A drop of blood appears.

"Well, how about that!" the man says. "Dead people *do* bleed!"

The man has a delusion but it's a fact as far as he's concerned. He should sound quite rational as he discusses it with the doctor. The doctor, equally, treats the delusion as quite normal.

A woman visits her doctor.

"Doctor," she says, "you know that Max and I are very happily married. But lately—I don't know—something is wrong. Frankly, his sexual appetites are stronger than mine; I love him as much as ever but I just can't live up to what he expects, and I feel sort of guilty about it. Is there any kind of thing that I could take, maybe?"

"Well," the doctor says, "matter of fact I've just been sent some samples of a new pill for that very thing. We don't know too much about it yet, but it does seem to produce the effect you're after. Look, I'll give you four; start off with just half a pill and see what the reaction is before you take a stronger dose."

A few days later the woman comes in again.

"Doctor, I've just come here to tell you that you've just about wrecked my marriage. That drug you gave me, why it's absolutely disgraceful—"

"What in the world happened? Didn't you do as I said?"

"Well, I must admit that it's partially my fault. I didn't take it at all until last night, about an hour and a half before dinner. I know you did say take just half a pill but—well, I disregarded your instructions and just took the whole four pills at once."

"Oh dear, oh dear," the doctor says, "and I suppose it had a very strong effect?"

"You may well ask. In the middle of dinner I suddenly got this impulse—absolutely violent. I didn't just want to make love to my husband—I practically raped him. I leaped up and dragged him onto the table—oh, it was simply awful—broke all the dishes, knocked over a bottle of wine, ruined the tablecloth—I've never behaved like that in my entire life!"

"But this is dreadful," the doctor says, "and even though you did disregard my instructions, I still feel at least partially to blame. I shouldn't have given you more than half a pill; it's really my fault. What can I do to make up for this? Look, I know it sounds silly but you did say that the dishes were broken, the wine spilled, tablecloth ruined; couldn't I at least pay for the damage?"

"Don't you give it a thought, Doctor—I'm quite sure they'll never let us in *that* restaurant again."

This story has quite a lot of dialogue and you're not expected to remember it word for word. Remember the form, the construction of the story and use dialogue to suit your own style. I've written it as I tell it. However, remember that the woman is serious, her problem is serious to her and it is to the doctor as well. Don't try for laughs before the end and avoid any appearance of sniggering over s—x.

A burglar is trying to get into a house. He tries all the doors and windows but no success. Now he's up on the second floor balcony. He looks in and sees a baby in a crib. By now he's pretty desperate so he talks to the baby:

"Oo-oo, bay-bee," he says, "itsy-bitsy poo, isn't oo gonna open window for nice mansie-wansie, hmmm?"

The baby says, "Ah, ya dumb bastard, I can't even *walk* yet!"

Naturally for this you must use a high, affected, talk-down-to-kiddie type of voice. The baby, on the other hand, has a gravelly bass, like Big Jule in Guys and Dolls. *The contrast is the key of the story. The "ah" of the baby is not the long "a" as in "father" but rather the short "a" as in "sack."*

A man, already a bit loaded, comes into a bar with his dog. He says to the bartender, "Look, Mac, I got a marvelous dog here—answers questions on any subject at all. Is it worth a straight scotch on the house if my dog answers a question?"

The bartender says, "Okay, I'll go for anything once."

He gives the man a scotch, the man drinks it and then says to the dog:

"Look, dog, pay attention now, 'cause this bartender's a real nice Joe. We wanna deliver, right? Okay, now. A man is building a house, see? He puts down a floor and puts up four walls. But he leaves something off, something very important. Now you tell 'im, dog, you tell 'im just what the man left off the house."

The dog goes, "R-r-r-rufff!"

"Hear that?" the drunk says. "Is that fantastic, hey? Howsabout another drink, Daddy-o, and my dog'll answer another question."

"I dunno," says the bartender, "I think there's a trick to it. All right, I'll go for it again."

He gives the man another drink. The man then says:

"Okay, now—pay real close attention, dog. Sammy Snead is teeing off on the golf course. Snead, mind you. He takes a swing at the ball and where does it go—down the fairway? No, sir, it does not. It goes away off to the left somewheres. Now, dog, you tell the bartender—where does that ball land?"

The dog goes, "R-r-r-rrufff!"

"See? See what I mean? Dog's a genius, eh? Howsabout another drink, Dad? One more drink and ole doggie here'll answer one more question."

The bartender says, "Let *me* ask the question."

"Sure, go on, *you* ask, whatsa difference who asks? That dog's an intellectual—really got it up here. So okay—you gimme the drink and *you* ask him a question."

He gets the drink. Then the bartender says:

"All right, dog—who was the greatest President the United States ever had?"

The dog goes, "R-r-r—McKinley?"

Again, here is a story that might telegraph the punch if you're not careful. It depends mainly on the dog. Each time he barks on the first two questions, he must make the same sound so that the listener thinks that's all the dog can do. Both on "roof" and "rough" his bark is the same, strictly "r-r-rufff."

You get the impression that the bartender has been swindled twice and is about to be again. On the third answer the dog begins his "r-r-r" growl as he did before but then cocks his head to one side, like the dog in the His Master's Voice ad and says, "McKinley?" in a clear though rather hesitant manner.

If you're telling this story out of the United States better use Eisenhower. Not Roosevelt because the name is not as much of a surprise, due to the first syllable being an "r" sound.

The drunk should be pleasantly loaded, always genial with his new-found sucker.

Make a contrast between the serious sobriety of the bartender and the mellow loaded contentment of the drunk.

At the first hole on a golf course a man tees off, hits a hard drive but the ball hooks badly and goes off the course entirely. The man figures it's a lost ball, puts another ball down and starts again. He plays nine holes when a policeman comes up to him:

"Sir, did you lose a ball awhile back?"

"Yes, I did. Why?"

"Well, sir, I'm afraid I've got bad news for you. You see, your ball struck a cyclist, causing him to swerve right into the path of an oncoming bus. The bus hit the cyclist but also rammed head-on into a truck coming from the opposite direction. At the moment the casualties are twenty-one dead and we don't know how many injured."

The man says, "But this is dreadful—I had no idea—is there anything that I can possibly do?"

"Well, sir, the next time you want to hold the club a little more to the right, like this—"

This story is told seriously all the way. The policeman is respectful but stern. The golfer grows increasingly agitated as the mishaps pile up. The policeman, of course, pantomimes his golf instructions at the end.

A man is at the roulette table in Monte Carlo. He's down to his last five hundred francs, so he decides to quit and use the five hundred for a taxi to his hotel. Just as he turns to leave the Casino he hears a mysterious voice, a sort of ghostly voice that seems to come from inside his own head. It says:

"*Le rouge.*"

"Wow," the man says to himself, "a hunch!" He goes back to the table, puts the five hundred on red. Red wins.

The voice says, "*Numéro douze.*"

He puts his money on twelve. Twelve wins. He goes to take the money and the voice says:

"*Numéro douze.*"

The man says, "Again?"

The voice says, "*Oui.*"

He leaves the money. Twelve wins again. The man quickly scoops up his winnings and starts to leave the table. The voice says:

"*Vingt-sept.*"

The man says, "But I'm ahead now!"

"*Vingt-sept.*"

"All of it?"

"*Oui.*"

So he puts the whole pile on twenty-seven. Nine wins. The voice says:

"*Ah, merde!*"

To my knowledge this story presents the only fallible ghost I've ever heard of. Usually these ghosts think they know everything. The ghost's voice is quietly authoritative, never gets excited, nor in any way human until the very last.

The man is at first delighted with his extra-sensory guide but from the moment he wins on twelve he wants to quit and get away. He bleats piteously at the ghost that he's ahead but ghost is inexorable.

The ghost is quietly exasperated at the last.

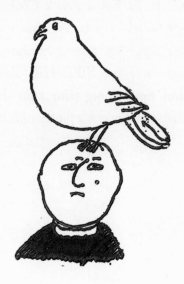

Some kids in the East End of London are playing marbles in a vacant lot. Some pigeons alight and are in the kids' way. One kid says:

"'Ere you, bugger off. C'mon now, bugger off."

A preacher just passing at that moment hears this. He comes over to the kids.

"Now children," he says, "that is no way to talk to the little birdies. Do you wish them to go away? Then you must say, 'shoo–shoo.' They'll bugger off."

The kid who speaks has a tough Cockney voice. The preacher is prissy, overly precise and has a naice refeened accent. He is the type that gets to conduct children's recreational programs over the BBC. His "shoo—shoo" is delivered slowly and almost sung with a lilt. He is still smiling and smarmy as he delivers his final words.

An American tourist is walking with his wife in Paris. They find a perfume shop, the wife goes in and he waits outside. A streetwalker comes along and says to him, in English:

"Like to come home with me, chéri?"

"For how much?" says the tourist.

"Five thousand francs."

"I'll give you five hundred."

The girl spits at him and says "Je vous dis 'merde.'" and walks away. A little later the man's wife comes out of the shop and they continue their walk. On the first corner they come to there is the same streetwalker. She takes one look at the man and his wife and says:

"You see? You see what you get for five hundred francs?"

What I've said before about accents I'll say again now. You need only a light French accent for the girl, a delicate "wiz" for "with" and a bit of a rolled "r" on "chéri." Avoid the grotesque.

If you're a non-American, be careful that you don't exaggerate the tourist. Far better to use your normal voice and accent in speaking English. American is very hard to do without falling into caricature, and the latter is a failing that will spoil almost any story.

The streetwalker's voice on her final speech is quite different from the wheedling one she used at first. Now she wants the neighbors to hear. She stands, legs apart, hands on hips, and nods contemptuously as she evaluates the wife.

Keep the dialogue as simple as possible. Again, you're not limited to mine, but don't lay on extra details.

You could simplify the girl's French phrase by merely having her spit and say, "Salaud."

A woman, coming out of a hotel, bumps into a man. The man steps back and says:

"I beg your pardon—hey—get a load of you—why, you must be the ugliest woman in the world!"

The woman says, "My good man, you're drunk."

"Quite true," the man says, "in fact, an understatement. I'm stinkin'! However—tomorrow I'll be sober. But you'll still be the *ugliest* woman in the world!"

There exists a tendency in telling this story, to attach it to someone in an effort to make it sound true. I have heard it told as a dialogue between Churchill and Bessie Braddock, a Labor MP in England, or told about the late Mrs. Roosevelt. I think the story as a story is funny. Put a name to the characters and it then becomes rather mean, a propaganda exercise.

The drunk should be polite and genial. He is imparting information, doesn't intend to be insulting. Nor does he

feel he's being insulted; he keeps his good humor through-
out, is almost euphoric as he says the last line. Avoid the
clichés of drunk behavior. No "hics," no weaving about and
just a slight slurring of speech.

A man comes from Czechoslovakia to live with his brother in New Jersey and gets a job in a munitions plant. He speaks no English and his brother teaches him to say "Apple pie and coffee" so that at least he can get something to eat at lunch time. But after about a fortnight apple pie and coffee are beginning to come out of his ears, and he begs his brother to teach him to say something else. His brother thinks for a while and says, "Okay, try this—chicken sandwich."

The brother says, "Tsee-ken sond-weets."

"That's great—you just say that tomorrow."

So the next day at lunch time, the man goes to the canteen. The waiter says, "Whaddia havin', Mac?"

"Tsee-ken sond-weets."

"Okay—hoddia wannit, white 'er rye, whole wheat 'er toast?"

The poor fellow bleats, "Tsee-ken sond-weets."

"Okay, okay, I hoidja the first time. C'mon now, Mac, ya holdin' evvybody up, hoddia wannit, white 'er rye, whole wheat 'er toast?"

(Gulp) "Opple pie und cawfee."

When the brother teaches the man to say "chicken sandwich" he should articulate it very slowly. He's teaching it, remember, to a man who speaks no English.

When he speaks to his brother conversationally, he is, naturally, speaking Czech so no accent is used.

There must be a sharp contrast between the gentle immigrant, trying to say phonetically the new phrase he has learned and the hard-boiled waiter who makes no concessions. The first time the man says "Tsee-ken sond-weets" he is fairly confident but when he is not understood and has to say it again he is not far from tears. There should be a fatalistic resignation in his voice as he gulps and asks for the dreaded apple pie and coffee.

A zebra is walking down a country lane in the United States. She sees some sheep in a field, comes up to the fence and calls to one of them:

"Excuse me, could I speak to you for just a moment? I represent the United Women Zebras of South Africa. I'm here on a fact-finding tour, to find out how American animals live and work. Would you care to tell me just what it is that you do?"

The sheep says, "What do I do? I give wool, what else?

When I grow enough wool, they shear it off and next season it's the same routine again. It's different in your country?"

"No, actually, quite the same. Well, thank you very much, you've been most kind."

Later on, farther down the road, she sees a cow.

"I beg your pardon, I'm from the United Women Zebras of South Africa. I've been delegated to interview American animals. Would you describe to me your functions as an American cow?"

"Not at all, I'm glad you asked me that. I'm a pure bred Guernsey, I give Grade A milk. All this pasture around here is for me and a few close friends. I live up there in that white barn—I'm sorry I can't ask you in but we're housecleaning and the place is just a shambles."

"I see. Well, thank you so much, you've been most helpful."

Later on she sees a stallion in a field. The stallion sees her, too. He comes charging toward the fence, comes to a four-footed skidding stop, and just looms over her with nostrils flaring. She looks up at him.

"And just what is it that *you* do?"

The stallion says, "Honey, you just slip out of that housecoat and I'll *show* you what I do!"

The zebra is a club-woman type, rather like the lioness in the musical story. She always sounds a shade patronizing, saying "veddy" for "very" and "Ameddican" for "American." She almost sings her sentences. She drops the club-woman manner when she speaks to the stallion and becomes coyly arch.

The sheep is an earthy New York type, rather below the zebra socially. He finds her questions a bit silly and his manner of answering, while polite, is a bit cynical. The cow, on the other hand, is flattered at being interviewed and tries hard to be helpful. The stallion, of course, knows what he wants and gets right to the point. He should sound more definite, more masculine and assertive than the other animals.

Some people like to say "pajamas" instead of "house-coat." Remember what I said about logic, that once the premise of a talking animal is accepted, the rest should be straightforward and logical. The zebra wouldn't be in pajamas, nor would the stallion think she was in them, it being broad daylight. "Housecoat" not only makes sense in the circumstances, but is to me a much funnier term and word picture.

Note also that the zebra's speech is different for each animal. This is to avoid monotony by repetition. Her question is basically the same each time but it is reworded. These little changes keep the line of the story fresher; the listener may not even notice that the dialogue is a bit different. If it were the same each time, however, he would notice that and might get bored with the story.

A rabbi is on his way to synagogue on Yom Kippur, the Day of Atonement. He passes his golf club on the way and feels that as it's very early in the morning and no one is around, it's quite safe to play a few holes. He goes to the locker room, gets his clubs, tees up a ball and starts taking a few practice swings. At this point Moses, who has been watching the whole thing from heaven, calls to God:

"Hey, Boss, look what's happening—you won't believe it. Here it is Yom Kippur and guess who's going to play golf —a rabbi!"

God says, "I know all about it. Who do you think you're talking to anyway? I not only know but don't you worry— I'm going to punish him."

The rabbi hits the ball, a beautiful drive, straight down the fairway, the ball lands on the green, drops into the cup, a hole in one.

Moses says, "Hey, what goes on here? A rabbi plays golf on Yom Kippur, you say you're going to punish him, and he makes a hole in *one!*"

God says, "So who can he tell?"

Moses and God are very matter-of-fact in their dialogue, a wee bit Bronxy. One warning: Moses' last speech is the pivot point of the story; make sure that everything he says is part of working up to the climax of God's answer. For example, don't let the word "so" appear anywhere in Moses' speech. If it does appear, it takes the edge off God saying, "So who can he tell?" Also, it should be quite clear in your opening description that the rabbi knows he's doing wrong but can't resist the urge.

A girl from the Lower East Side in New York marries a Gentile who lives on Park Avenue. After her marriage she takes Momma to live with her and Momma speaks nothing but Yiddish. Daughter gets a tutor to teach Momma to speak English and after about a year, daughter thinks Momma is ready to attend dinner parties. So at her next party, there is Momma sitting at the table, looking very elegant in black bombazine, wearing a new *sheitel* (wig) but for a long time saying nothing at all. Suddenly Momma turns to the man at her right and begins talking to him in Yiddish. The daughter is mortified and she taps on the table to try to get Momma's attention:

"Mumsie, remember what you promised? Nothing but English, remember?"

The old lady nods, turns again to the man on her right and with terrible clarity says:

"You a no-good Fascist anti-Semite bastard. *Ist gut gesagt?*"

96

When the daughter speaks to Momma, she is affectedly elegant, as in her use of "Mumsie" rather than "Momma." She should talk as if she sported a lorgnette. Her "s" sounds are almost lisped, very sibilant. Momma should smile very graciously as she insults the guest on her right but should beam amiably at her daughter as she goes back into Yiddish, which she does without a pause after "anti-Semite bastard." The Yiddish means, "Is that said well?" Maybe—a big maybe—you could say the last part in English, in which case you'd say, "Did I say it good?" Try to use the Yiddish punch line, though. "Gesagt" is pronounced "gezogt."

In Bowery night court there are three girls charged with soliciting in the street and one man arrested for operating a pushcart without a license. First, one of the girls comes before the judge.

"Your Honor," she says, "I was just walking along with my friend here when a man asked me did I have a match. *Well,* the next thing I knew, this officer appeared and *ooh,* the *things* he *said!* Perfectly *disgraceful,* and I mean, how anybody could even *think* such a thing—"

The judge looks at the charge sheet.

"Doreen LaRue," he says, "I find here that you've had three previous convictions for soliciting. I shall have to fine you thirty dollars or six days in jail. Next case."

The second girl says, "Your Honor, it's exactly like she says. We're both private secretaries, a perfectly *respectable* occupation and if our mothers ever so much as *dreamed* that we were in this court, they'd *die* of shame, they really *would.*"

The judge says, "Lizzie Belle, you've had five previous

convictions on the same charge—soliciting. That'll be fifty dollars or ten days in jail. Next?"

The third girl says, "Judge, I'm a whore. I'm not proud of it especially, but that's what I am and that's about the only way for me to make a buck."

"Young lady," the judge says, "in all my years on the bench you're the first honest woman to come before this court. Your case is dismissed. Oh, and Sergeant, make out a contribution for this young lady of twenty-five dollars from the Policemen's Fund. Next case?"

The old fellow arrested for operating a pushcart comes up.

"Your Honor," he says, "what's the use trying to fool a learned man like you. I'm a whore."

There is a danger in this story of your listener anticipating the punch line. You have to pay a lot of attention to the characters in the buildup so that it appears that the girls are the main part of the story. The pushcart man should be forgotten about until he makes his appearance at the end of the story.

The girls should be Bronx voices but aiming at supergentility in their speech, rather like Brenda and Cobyna on Bob Hope's radio show of some years ago. The first two girls, that is. The third girl speaks without affectation, no alibi, no self-pity. The man takes his cue from the third girl: what's good enough for her is good enough for him. No oiliness, no wheedling. Slight Yiddish accent, but very slight.

A mother persuades Jascha Heifetz to listen to her nine-year-old boy play the violin. The kid saws his way through the first movement of the Mendelssohn concerto. When he finishes, Heifetz turns to the boy's mother:

"Your son has a rather *small* tone—but *very* disagreeable."

This is the kind of story that tempts the teller to add details. It's tempting, for example, to give the mother some dialogue but it doesn't help the story, which depends on the tone of voice used by Heifetz. He raises the expectation of qualified praise and then delivers an uppercut. Heifetz seems a bit apologetic on the first part of the sentence but smiles cordially as he says, "but very disagreeable."

Mike Todd arrives at the gates of Heaven. St. Peter says:

"Mike, baby, are we glad you're here! We're all set to put on a great show—Mike, baby, when you see the script you'll flip!—and we've just been waiting for you!"

Todd says, "Wait a minute, what's all the rush? I haven't even got my coat off yet. Whaddya mean, you're waiting for *me*? You got some great guys up here—Ziegfeld, Hammerstein, Shubert, De Mille—"

"Yeah, yeah, sure, they're here all right and they're great like you say. But Mike, baby, we need a guy who thinks *big*, know what I mean?"

"Well, okay, I don't want to let you guys down, but let's get one thing straight right away. I work up here like I worked down there, y'understand? Complete authority—no kibitzing—nobody, but *no*body, tells me what to do. You dig?"

"Crazy!—you're in charge."

So Mike goes to work. He rehearses an aerial ballet with three hundred angels doing triple loops and Immelmann turns. He has Gabriel doing three solo choruses. ("Look, baby, you're great, doll, but a little on the square side. That Clyde McCoy stuff is out, man—you want those Dizzy licks, y'understand, loverboy?")

After about three weeks rehearsal St. Peter comes around.

"Mike," he says, "look, I don't want you to get the idea I'm reneging or anything. I promised you complete autonomy and you got to admit I've kept my word, eh, baby? It's just that—well—the Boss was wondering, have you got a part in the show for his son?"

Everybody talks a combination of Broadway and hip in this one, even St. Peter. Mike should be a tough, cigar-in-mouth New York type. This story allows plenty of room for improvisation. I like angels doing Hollywood-type stunt ballets and Gabriel being taught to play like Gillespie but you may have better ideas. St. Peter in his last speech is very diffident. He's reluctant, afraid of ruffling the great man, but he's got to do what the Boss tells him.

A New York agent auditions a singer. Her name is Bertha Braunschweig, she has a beak like a parrot and a very strong Bronx accent. He listens through one chorus, then he says:

"Look, honey, you're a nice kid but show business ain't for you, believe me. Go back to the Bronx, marry a doctor, be happy. Forget about show business, I'm telling you what I'd tell my own daughter."

About three years later he receives an invitation to come to the opening, at the Waldorf, of a new singer, Pamela Brunswick. He goes, and when Miss Brunswick comes out for her first number he is amazed because he recognizes Bertha Braunschweig. She's had a great nose job, her hair is carefully set and her gown is not only in excellent taste, she wears it like a Dior mannequin, but there's no doubt about it, this is Bertha. And when she begins to sing, the diction is elegant.

"Get-ting to know you—get-ting to know you but nice-ly
  You are pr-r-rrecise-ly *mein gless* of tea."

I think that Bertha need only be described, not demonstrated. If you must *demonstrate*, make sure you have a good Bronx accent and sing about eight bars of, say, "April in Paris," then have the agent interrupt with his "Look, honey" lines.

Bertha as Pamela, of course, is near-British (phony British, of course). She sings mincingly, with pursed mouth and fluttering eyelids. She rolls the "r" of "precisely," all of which sets the scene for the anticlimax of "mein gless" where she lapses into Yiddish accent but still with the British facial mannerisms.

Two men are going up in the cable car ski lift at Klosters, in Switzerland. One has never been before.

"Hey," he says, "this thing looks dangerous. Big heavy car attached to that skinny little wire. Suppose it breaks?"

"It won't break."

"Wise guy, it won't break! Look down there, a coupla thousand feet drop, and Mr. Knowitall, he's so sure it won't break."

"Look, I've been on this thing a million times. Anyway, that's not a wire, it's a thick cable. And even, God forbid, it should break, you're still in no danger. There's an auxiliary cable, so the first cable breaks, except it never breaks, but *if* it breaks, automatically the car is caught by the auxiliary cable."

"What if the electricity fails?"

"It never fails."

"Oh sure, it never fails. There couldn't be a first time? The current fails, look at the slanty angle, we go sliding backward, we get hit against the mountain and goodbye Cholly."

"Look, you can't see it from here but they got an emergency brake. Anything goes wrong, the emergency brake goes on right away, automatically. So stop worrying already."

"And if the brake don't take hold?"

"They've thought of that. Behind the first emergency brake they got a *second* emergency brake so the first brake goes wrong, zoom, it takes over in a jiffy the second emergency brake."

"So what if they both fail?"

The friend gets desperate.

"Look—on top of this car, you can't see, but they got two steel claws. In *case* both emergency brakes don't work, this is already absolutely impossible, but just in case, the two steel claws come together and grip tight the cable, the car is held in position until a rescue car comes up. You're in no danger whatsoever."

"And if the claws don't grip?"

The friend says, "Oh, you can kiss my ass."

A stranger says, "He could've kissed *mine* at the second emergency brake."

A Jewish inflection rather than a strong accent. The two men are the same types as in the finger-bowl story, one is strong-voiced and confident, the other a little Milquetoast, (albeit a Jewish Milquetoast). Here, again, you must time the punch line very carefully so that you don't get a false finish. If they laugh on "Oh, you can kiss my ass," it will be because you have given them the impression that the story has ended, which makes it nothing more than a chance to use the semi-verboten expression. The stranger must come in with his line hard on "kiss my ass" to insure the true finish.

The pessimist starts a pessimist and remains one, never satisfied. The friend is patient but loses his calm at the continual nagging.

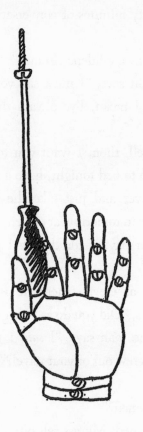

A man goes to see a psychiatrist who asks him the reason for the visit.

"Well," the man says, "it's my friends, really. They're worried about this screw I have in my navel. It doesn't bother me at all but it does bother my friends so, just to please them, I made an appointment to see you."

After about forty minutes of conversation the psychiatrist says:

"Do you have any confidence in me?"

"Well," the man says, "I must say you're different from what I expected. I mean, I've always thought you fellows were crackpots."

"I see. Very well, then, I want you to do something for me. When you go to bed tonight, have a screwdriver handy; take the screwdriver and just take the screw *out* of your navel. Then, come in tomorrow at eleven, okay?"

"Very well. I'm paying for this so I may as well do as you say."

Next morning at eleven there he is. The psychiatrist greets him and says, "Did you do as I suggested?"

"Of course," the man says, "I *said* I would, and I *did*."

"You took the screw out of your navel?"

"Yes."

"So what happened?"

"So what happened! My *ass* fell off!"

The patient is a bit prissy, impatient of all psychiatrists. If you can remember Edward Everett Horton, he's a bit like that. The doctor is cordial, good-humored. When the patient returns the next morning his manner suggests that although he had begun to think maybe there was something to this psychiatry business, he's back to his original opinion—they're all crackpots. He gets more and more impatient with the doctor, finally exploding the punch line with a near-feminine (but not swish) burst of indignation.

A man goes to see his doctor.

"Doc," he says, "I got a funny kind of problem. When the wife and me was first married, it was really great, know what I mean? Really had the old b'zazz, the old *uh-voom*. But lately, I dunno, it kinda lacks something—I don't know how to say it, Doc—but to be absolutely frank, the whole thing's kinda, well, *boring*. No excitement, none of the old *uh-voom!*"

The doctor says, "How long've you been married?"

"Be thirty years next month and, I dunno, it just ain't the same as it used to be. Maybe it's my fault, maybe it's hers but, I dunno, I get kinda lackadaisical about it, know what I mean?"

"Well, you know," the doctor says, "you can't expect that honeymoon rapture to last forever. Thirty years, after all, that's a long time. I don't know what to tell you—can't think of anything specific—no, wait a minute, there's one thing you might do."

"You just tell me, Doc, and I'll try it—anything to get back the old *uh-voom!*"

"Well, look then," the doctor says, "you've said yourself that sex has become sort of routine with you. Maybe you even have a fixed schedule?"

"Well, yeah, Doc, now that you mention it, yeah, we got a schedule. Every second Friday, ten o'clock P.M."

"Well then, why don't you try surprise? I mean, don't wait for the second Friday? Why not just when the impulse hits you? Right then and there, and well, I don't guarantee anything, but it just might work. Try it, anyway."

"Sure, Doc, anything you say. And I'll letcha know how it works out."

He comes back the next day.

"Well, Doc, I took your advice. In fact, I was thinking about it all the way home, I thought to myself, that Doc's a shrewd cookie, he really knows. And the whole idea, the more I thought of it, the better it sounded and I started to get all worked up. And I figured, it's Thursday, she won't be expecting anything unusual and—well, by that time I was home. I rang the bell, I didn't have my key, and my wife answered the door. I came in and you know, Doc, our entrance hall—well, the dining room's just off the hall, see? So I says to myself, hell, why not right now, hey? So before my wife can figure out what's happening, I just grabbed her and pushed her into the dining room, right onto the table and boy, it was great! And the whole time I'm thinking to myself, that Doc's a killer, he's really on the ball. But then, after a while, I dunno, the whole thing got kinda mechanical, and the old b'zazz wasn't there any more—none of that old *uh-voom*, know what I mean? Just kinda boring. But I'll say one thing—it made a *hell* of a hit with our dinner guests."

As with any story involving sex, avoid the smirk or the leer. This fellow isn't telling a smoking-car story—he's talking about a serious problem. He's an amiable Babbitt, a nice but dull guy, and he tells his story in a relaxed almost indifferent manner. He comes temporarily to life as he describes "the old b'zazz, the old uh-voom," *and he gives an imaginary punch with clenched fist for emphasis. But he soon relapses. As he says himself, he's kind of lackadaisical. (Don't know what to call him but he's mighty lackadaisical.) And he brings out the last line not as a climax, not as any kind of triumph, but just to let the doctor know that some good came from taking his advice.*

An analyst says to his patient:

"You know, for the past few months we've been working on the theory that you have a deep-rooted inferiority complex. Well, I've got good news for you—we can dispense with that treatment. You have *no* inferiority complex— you're *really inferior!*"

The analyst is dead serious and is genuinely happy as he delivers the good news to his patient.

A man comes for his first visit to a psychiatrist. He seems deeply depressed, doesn't react much to anything. The psychiatrist decides to test him to see if he has any of the more obvious fetishes. He shows him a collection of shoes, all kinds of shoes. No reaction. He shows him a case containing whips, chains, knives, spikes. Nothing. Then the psychiatrist opens a closet full of women's evening dresses. The patient's eyes light up and he reaches out for one. The psychiatrist slaps his hand.

"Don't you *dare* touch that one—it's *mine!*"

This one is a bit contrived, what with those various collections, so it's not one of my favorites. Still, it has a nice twist at the finish. The psychiatrist camps a bit, of course, but don't overdo it.

The *alte yentes* (literally, old aunts, but refers to gossipy elderly women) are discussing their sons:

"Mein boy, Leopold, is that a boy! You know what he does? Comes wintertime, he sends me for a fortnight to Miami Beach. You know what else? He arranges, at the airport should meet me a nice young man, for the whole two weeks is mein escort, I shouldn't be on my own, I shouldn't have nowhere to go. Everything is fixed up in advance, I go to all the night clubs, see all the best floor shows, that's mein Leopold."

The second *yente* says, "That's very nice, very nice indeed, he's a good boy, you should be proud. But let me tell you about mein Stanley. Stanley wants too his Momma should have it a coupla weeks at Miami but Stanley doesn't *send* Momma, he *takes* Momma to Miami. And Stanley, he don't want no stranger should take his Momma around, Stanley takes *personally* his Momma to the beach, to the movies, to the night clubs. Oo, I could eat him up, he's such a wonderful boy, mein Stanley."

The third mother says, "Well, you both of you, you got

two fine boys there, no doubt about it. Very good boys indeed. But you know mein Irving? Let me tell you about Irving. Mein Irving, he goes every day, six days a week, to a man, fifty dollars each time Irving pays him and Irving lies down on a couch and talks. And do you know what he talks about? Me!"

Naturally, these are Yiddishe Mommas. The dialogue has Yiddish feeling but not a thick accent. These are well-to-do Mommas. They're proud of their boys and the pride grows from mother to mother. The second mother should sound a bit more prissy than the first, a bit like Adelaide in Guys and Dolls. *She is just a shade malicious as she points out that "Stanley takes* personally *his Momma," etc. And "personally" should be rather ritzily intoned.*

The third Momma really believes she's scoring on the others and there should be a note of rather complacent triumph in her final "Me!" A shorter form of this story is the Momma who tells her friend that her son has an Oedipus complex. The friend says, "Oedipus, schmoedipus, so long as he loves his mother!"

Two horses in adjoining stalls at a racing stable. One horse says:

"Fred, I've had something on my mind lately—it's worrying me a lot. Fred, I don't know if you've heard, but there's a rumor that I'm going to be sold. I haven't done too well my last few times out. Well, I'm used to it here and I'd hate to have to start all over again somewhere else, some strange stable. Now Fred—I don't quite know how to say this—it's very embarrassing—but it so happens we're both running in the same race tomorrow. Now, I'm not asking anything irregular, mind you, you understand that—but Fred—if I could come in a winner for just that one race—"

The other horse says, "Bert, I sympathize with you completely. I know just how you feel and frankly, I'd hate to see you leave. But Bert, what you're asking—well, in a way, you're asking me to violate my own code of ethics as a race horse. Bert, I'd do anything in the world for you but—"

A bulldog, lying at their feet, looks up and says, "Look, Fred, is it gonna kill you if Bert wins one race?"

One horse says, "Get a load of that—a *talking dog!*"

Bert is hesitant, rather whiny in his approach. Fred is manly—or horsy—and both are very sincere. Fred hates to turn down his pal and is working up a lather of righteousness when he is interrupted by the bulldog, who sounds a bit cynical, fed up with Fred's mealymouthed ethics. The horse is just astonished as he blurts out his final line.

On a transatlantic liner, during the ship's concert, a magician is doing his act, and notices a woman staring rather disapprovingly at him. On his last trick he says, "Now for the highlight of my act: I'm going to make the whole ship disappear!" At that moment there's a terrific explosion in the boiler room and in just a few minutes the ship has sunk. The magician is in the water, holding on to a piece of wood when the woman who was staring at him comes swimming past. She looks at the magician and says:

"Whatsa matter with you, you some kinda *nut?*"

Don't add details to this one, keep it short. The woman not only thinks the magician is lousy, the last trick proves it to her.

A man goes to see a psychiatrist. "I have this illusion," he says. "I don't have it all the time, but every once in awhile I get this very strong feeling that I'm a dog."

The psychiatrist says, "Well, whatever it is, we'd better investigate. Would you please lie down on the couch?"

The man says, "Oh, I'm not allowed on the couch."

As in any story dealing with a mental aberration, the patient is very serious and you, the story-teller, do not make fun of him.

A man goes to a brothel. He says to the madam:

"I want you to know in advance, I'm a terrible man, a monster, absolutely a perverted fellow. I like to beat women and I have my own whip specially made for me. Can you do anything for a terrible person like me?"

The madam says, "Oh, sure, we get all types, but beating, that comes pretty high. You'll have to give the girl a hundred dollars."

"Well, it's high, like you say, but what am I going to do? I'm a depraved man, so I got to gratify my vicious desires, no matter what it costs."

He picks out a girl and they go upstairs. He gives her a hundred dollars and then begins to beat her. After a while she says:

"Hey, how long does this go on?"

He says, "'Til you give back the hundred dollars."

In spite of what the man says about himself he should be rather shy, a bit naïve. He is diffident when he speaks to the madam and just as diffident when he answers the girl.

123

A chimpanzee comes into a bar, orders a martini and puts down a ten-dollar bill. The bartender goes back to the cash register and speaks to his boss. "Hey," he says, "get a load of what just ordered a martini."

The boss looks. "Hey, how 'bout that!"

The bartender says, "That's not all—he gave me this ten. Whaddia think?"

The boss says, "Aah, give him a buck change, see what happens. He prolly won't know the difference."

The bartender serves the drink and puts down a dollar bill change. He says to the chimp, "You new 'round here?"

The chimp says, "Yup."

"Yeh, I kinda thought you was. Y'know, we don't get many chimpanzees comin' in here."

The chimp says, "At nine dollars for a martini, I'm not surprised."

I have already stressed that stories about talking animals should be logical, as if the animals were human. In this story it's the chimpanzee who has dignity. The bartender and his boss are gyp artists and the bartender is a hypocrite as well, with his false friendliness to the chimp. The chimpanzee's final line is said calmly but a bit scornfully. He sees through these jerks, but he's above making an issue over money.

Two girls meet on the beach at Miami. One says:

"So what's new?"

The other says, "Wait'll you hear! I was at the doctor's this morning, he gives me an examination, and you know what he says? He says I'm gradually turning into a man."

"So what *else* is new?"

These are Bronx-type girls. The "s's" are sibilant, conso-nants very exaggerated. "Turning" is somewhere between "toining" and "tuhning." "Taining" is somewhere near it. She is "grad-you-al-ly taining ginto a man," and "man" is somewhat like "may-yun." The girl who asks the questions has the same accent but she sounds bored with life.

A man passes a pet shop, hears a canary, comes into the shop and says he wants to buy the bird. Just as the proprietor is about to wrap up the cage the man says:

"Hey, wait a minute, I just noticed—that canary's got only one leg."

The canary says, "Look, Mac, whaddya want—a singer or a dancer?"

The bird, a tough guy, has learned his English watching TV serials.

A man buys a canary. When the shopkeeper hands him the cage the man says, "Look, that sparrow in the cage with the canary—take him out, will you?"

The storekeeper says, "The sparrow goes with the canary."

"But I don't want the sparrow. Who needs a sparrow? Take him out and just give me the canary."

"Mister, I ain't charging you nothing extra. The sparrow goes with the canary, in fact I may as well tell you, if you want the canary, you *gotta* take the sparrow."

"But this is ridiculous! The canary sings great, I want the canary, so why, for Christ's sake, do I *have* to take the sparrow?"

"The sparrow's his arranger."

The customer grows more and more impatient as the sparrow is being forced upon him. The storekeeper is deadpan, rather resigned, and gives the impression that he's been through all this many times before. Keep the dialogue between customer and shopkeeper strictly to the point. You act out both parts, of course, and don't let down on either one, because the dialogue builds, grows in momentum, to the slightly shaggy-dog point.

A woman has her husband's body cremated and has the ashes put in an urn which she puts on the piano in the living room. She doesn't tell her friends what it is and they get into the habit of tapping their cigarettes into it. One day, about six months later, she's doing some spring cleaning. She picks up the urn and says to her maid, "I know you're gonna think I'm crazy, but I could swear Sam's putting on weight."

Nothing special needed for this one. It makes me think of the actor who said in his will that he wanted to be cremated and have 10 per cent of his ashes thrown in his agent's face.

A woman wakes up in the middle of the night and feels that there's something in the room with her. She sees, silhouetted against the window, a man wearing an opera cloak. He starts toward her and she can see that instead of teeth he has fangs. Well, she's read her *Dracula* and she knows that there's one sure protection against vampires. She has a crucifix right by her bed; she grabs it and thrusts it out at him. He keeps coming toward her. She jumps to the foot of the bed and holds the crucifix right in front of his face. He says:

"Honeybunch, it vouldn't do you a *bit* of good."

This, so far as I know, is the only Jewish vampire. He's very friendly, bears no ill will and he should smile with the geniality of a waiter at a Jewish restaurant as he speaks his line. Slight Yiddish accent, naturally.

A prize fighter goes in to see his manager.

"I want a fight," he says, "I'm really ready now. Look at 'at footwork, hey? C'mon now, watch 'at left jab. Hoddya like that, hey? The ole reflexes, great! So, I want a fight, see?"

The manager says, "Sure, if you feel you're ready, I'll get you a fight. Got any ideas about who you'd like to fight?"

"Yeah, I know *just* who I wanna fight. I wanna fight Kid Robinson."

The manager says, "Look, if I've told you once, I've told you a million times. *You're* Kid Robinson!"

The usual punchy boxer mannerisms. He keeps weaving as he talks, constantly thumbs the side of his nose. New York Eighth Avenue accent, rather like William Bendix. The manager is patient, quietly resigned. He's been through this before.

A wealthy Negro couple employs a Jewish butler. One evening during dinner, the Negro says to his butler: "Would you bring in a bottle of a '59 Beaujolais." The butler goes out singing:

> *"Press* 'at grape an' *cul*tivate the vine
> We're gonna *dig* that *vin*tage fifty-nine—*crazy!"*

The Negro says to his wife, "You've got to hand it to those Jews, they sure got rhythm!"

You need no pronounced accents in this one. The Negro speaks normally, the Jew is a Village hipster. You'll have to make up your own tune; the first line of "I've Got Shoes" would fit fairly well. Main thing is, make it sound like a jazz lick, and have the Jew snap his fingers as he goes away singing.

A Negro gets off a bus at Madison Avenue and 49th Street in New York. He says to a man on the corner:

"Hey, Daddy, is this 48th and Madison?"

The man says: "No, this is 49th. You want 48th, you got to go down one block. You've come one block too far north."

"You sure about that, Daddy?"

"Of course I'm sure. I live around here. This is 49th, see? You want 48th, don't you? Well, you've come one block too far, you want to walk down one block, see where that drugstore is? That's it."

"Well, I mean, now, you *positive?*"

"You're damned right I'm positive. You want 48th, don't you? You're on 49th, right? How many times do I have to tell you, you're a block past it!"

"Hey, what'd you just call me, Daddy?"

This is an "in" story and would go very well, I should think, with the show biz crowd, musicians, people in general who understand the idiocy of prejudice well enough to make jokes about it.

The Negro is very hip, the white is an average New York type. The white gets more and more impatient as the Negro persists in questioning his directions. Forgive me for spelling c-a-t but the penultimate line should sound like "you're a black bastard." Even when the Negro misunderstands that crack, his own reaction is more incredulous than menacing.

A Negro sits down at a table at a very chic restaurant. The waiter comes up with a menu.

"I don't need no menu," the man says, "I know what I want. You got any chittlins?"

The waiter says, "Pardon?"

"Chittlins."

"One moment, sir, I will inquire." He goes away, comes back and says, "No, sir, we do not have that word that you have said."

"Got any hominy grits?"

"No, I am quite certain not, sir."

"What about hogback and melon?"

"Oh, I could give you melon, sir—would you like it with prosciutto?"

The man says, "Kee-rist!", gets up and starts to leave. The head waiter comes running after him.

"Excuse me, sir, isn't everything to your liking?"

The man says, "Hell, man, this restaurant ain't *ready* for integration!"

The Negro speaks in a strong assertive manner. The waiter has a French accent but very slight. The Negro is fairly patient until he is offered prosciutto but his "Kee-rist!" after that conveys complete disgust. The same disgusted tone, though with even more vigor, in the final line.

A man is sitting at a table in a French restaurant. The waiter brings him a menu. The man says:

"I'll begin with the *pampelmousse*. Then a *potage St. Germain*, the *caneton à l'orange*, with *petits pois* and *haricots verts*. No dessert. I'll have coffee espresso, and would you send me the wine waiter, please?"

The waiter is writing busily on his pad. When he finishes, he tears off the piece of paper and sets it down in front of the customer, then goes off. The man picks up the paper and finds the waiter has written:

"Sir; your fly is open. Two ladies just to your right have been ogling you. When I return with the *pampelmousse* I will stand between you and the ladies long enough to give you a chance to adjust your clothing. PS—I love you."

L1